FUNNY PLANTS

By Paul Mason and Tony De Saulles

First published in Great Britain in 2024
by Wayland

Text and Design Copyright © Hodder and Stoughton, 2024
Illustrations Copyright © Tony De Saulles, 2024

All rights reserved.

Editor: Grace Glendinning
Designer: Peter Scoulding
Consultant: Dr Max Coleman, Science Communicator,
Royal Botanic Garden Edinburgh

HBK ISBN: 978 1 5263 2289 0
PBK ISBN: 978 1 5263 2290 6
EBK ISBN: 978 1 5263 2584 6

Printed and bound in China

Wayland, an imprint of
Hachette Children's Group
Part of Hodder and Stoughton
Carmelite House
50 Victoria Embankment
London EC4Y 0DZ

An Hachette UK Company
www.hachette.co.uk
www.hachettechildrens.co.uk

London Borough of Enfield	
91200000825003	
Askews & Holts	14-Nov-2024
J580 JUNIOR NON-FICT	
ENBUSH	

The website addresses (URLs) included in this book were valid at the time of going to press. However, it is possible that contents or addresses may have changed since the publication of this book. No responsibility for any such changes can be accepted by either the author or the Publisher.

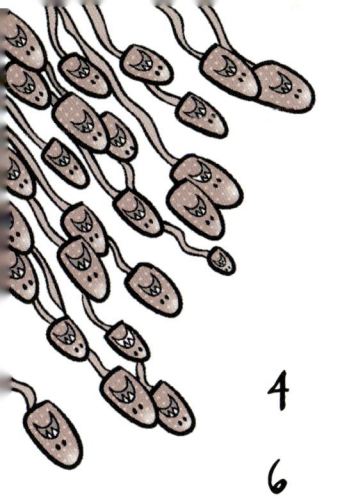

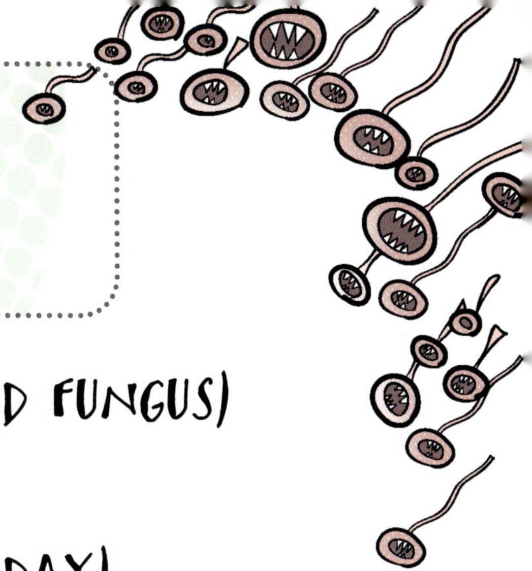

CONTENTS

4 THE CRAZY WORLD OF PLANTS (AND FUNGUS)
6 WHEN PLANTS EXPLODE!
8 GLOWING IN THE DARK (AND THE DAY)
10 PLANTS THAT ATTACK
12 PLANTS THAT MOVE IT
14 COMPLETE STINKERS
16 VERY FUNNY FUNGI
18 FRUIT IS FUNNY, TOO
20 TRICKSTER PLANTS
22 SHAPELY PLANTS
24 TERRIFIC TREES
26 PLANTS AND PEOPLE
28 MORE FUNNY PLANTS
30 PLANTS QUIZ
31 GLOSSARY
32 INDEX

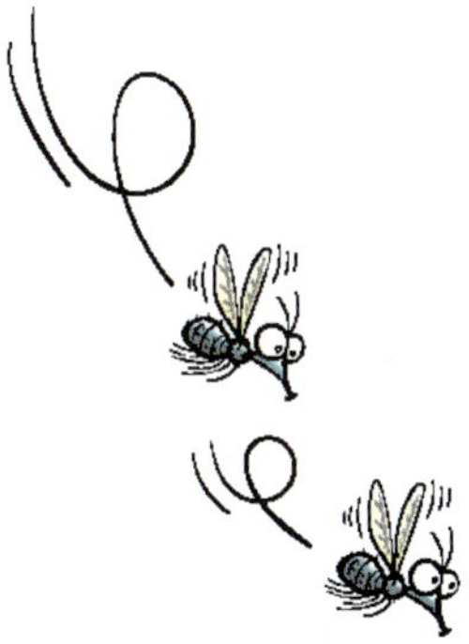

THE CRAZY WORLD OF PLANTS (AND FUNGUS)

Look around — how many plants can you see nearby? Are any of them as funny-looking as the plants on these pages?

'ELLO!

Some plants are funny because they just look funny.

Hydnora, for example, looks like a large, gaping, red mouth.

Or the sausage tree, guaranteed to drive any passing dogs crazy with hunger ... until they taste one of the 'sausages'.

YUM!

I SAID, "WHAT'S YOUR NAME?"

Eek, what happened to YOU?

There are even plants that look like parrots, tortoises or cobras.

HISSS!

Other plants are funny because of how they behave ... or smell.

Imagine meeting a cucumber that squirted seeds at you, for example.

Some cucumber species have no manners.

← Squirting cucumber

Some cucumber species are NO FUN!

KA-PLOOSH!

← Salad cucumber

Or a plant that smells like dead meat.

Who me?

One of the two stars of this book are fungi.
These are not actually plants at all — they have their own category.

But look at them! They are simply too much fun to miss out.

Thanks for including us!

Of course, plants and fungi don't really have eyes, but imagine what they would see if they DID — and the expressions they would pull!

5

WHEN PLANTS EXPLODE!

A few plants have found an extreme way to spread their seeds — by exploding like a firework.

SQUIRTING CUCUMBER

Explodes like: a roman candle

One touch and this sensitive fruit drops off its stalk — and out spurts a stream of sticky, seed-carrying liquid. Watch out!

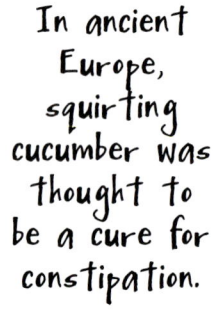

In ancient Europe, squirting cucumber was thought to be a cure for constipation.

Unnng! Please let it be true!

TOUCH-ME-NOTS

Explodes like: a rocket

When this plant is ready to release its seeds, a tiny touch — from an insect or a drop of water — causes the seed pod to explode, like a rocket going off.

Looks like rain...

Aaah! BAM!

What just happened?

BUNCHBERRY DOGWOOD

Explodes like: a box of fireworks

Come near and the bunchberry explodes, showering you with pollen. It all happens too fast to see, even for fast-moving flies.

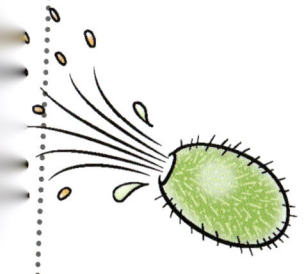

Let's rest here...

BOOM!

This is getting ridiculous!

7

GLOWING IN THE DARK (AND THE DAY)

Plants that could light your way in the dark? You'd better believe it.

FOXFIRE FUNGUS

These fungi usually live as long strands hidden inside rotten or dying trees. When they do show up outside, they come as quite a surprise: they glow in the dark.

Centuries ago their ghostly light was named foxfire and was used to light up the controls on early submarines.

WHERE'S MY BOX OF FOXFIRE FUNGUS?

It's so dark I can't find it, captain!

GHOST PIPE

In the deepest, darkest forests, ghost pipes shine like ... well, like ghost plants. Because there's no sunlight, the plants steal their food from a fungus in the soil.

Stop crowding me!

MOVE over!

Don't worry — there's plenty of fungus for everyone.

SLURP!

ANY PLANT, PERHAPS?

In 2020, scientists did an experiment. They injected ordinary plants with material from glow-in-the-dark mushrooms. The result? Glow-in-the-dark plants! Imagine what you could make glow in your life ...

PLANTS THAT ATTACK

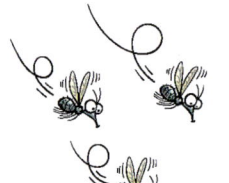

Most plants live on sunshine, air and water, but some live on meat.

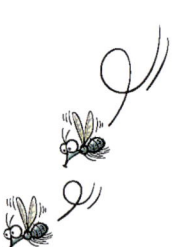

VENUS FLYTRAP

Speed: too fast to see

The Venus flytrap is a ticking bomb. When a fly touches a hair on the inside of the leaf, a 20-second timer starts. If it touches another hair before the timer stops ... SNAP!

The leaves close together in a tenth of a second.

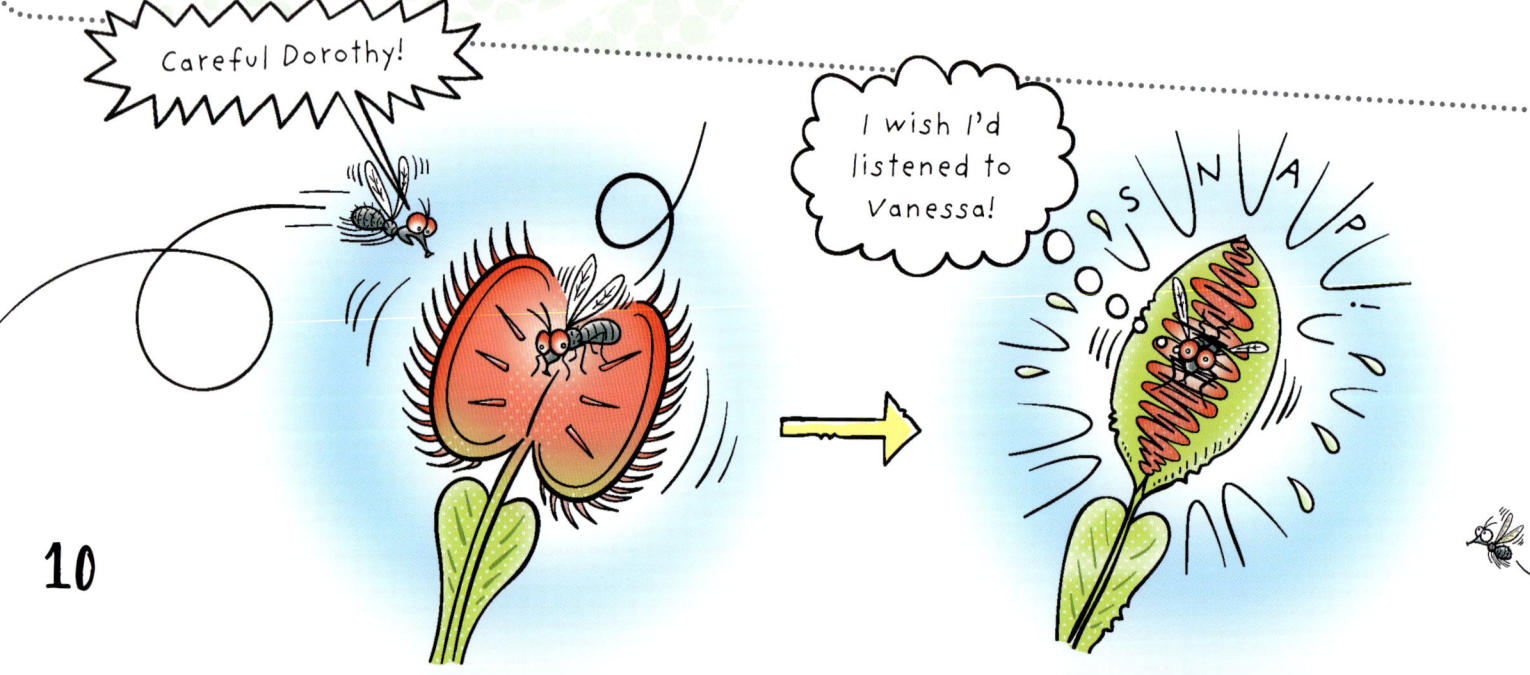

SNAP!

Careful Dorothy!

I wish I'd listened to Vanessa!

10

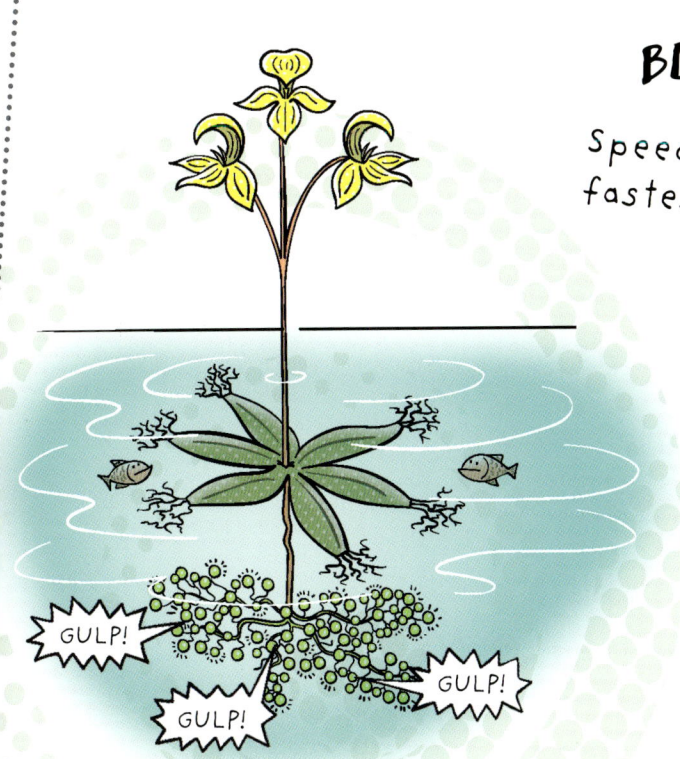

BLADDERWORT

Speed: top (said to be the fastest plant on Earth)

This water plant waits for tiny crustaceans to touch little hairs on a trapdoor. WHOOSH! The trapdoor opens and the crustacean is sucked in.

GULP! GULP! GULP!

Woah! Is this some sort of cave?

Nope! It's my mouth!

GULP!

CAPE SUNDEW

Speed: really quite slow

The Cape sundew is in no rush for its dinner. The plant slowly bends its tentacles toward its stuck victim until it is completely wrapped up.

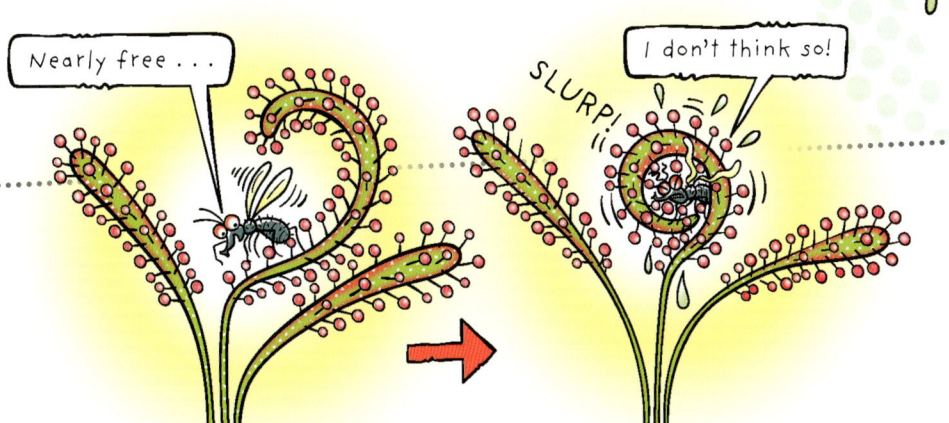

SLURP!

Nearly free...

SLURP!

I don't think so!

PLANTS THAT MOVE IT

All plants move, even if only by growing.
But some plants REALLY know how to move it.

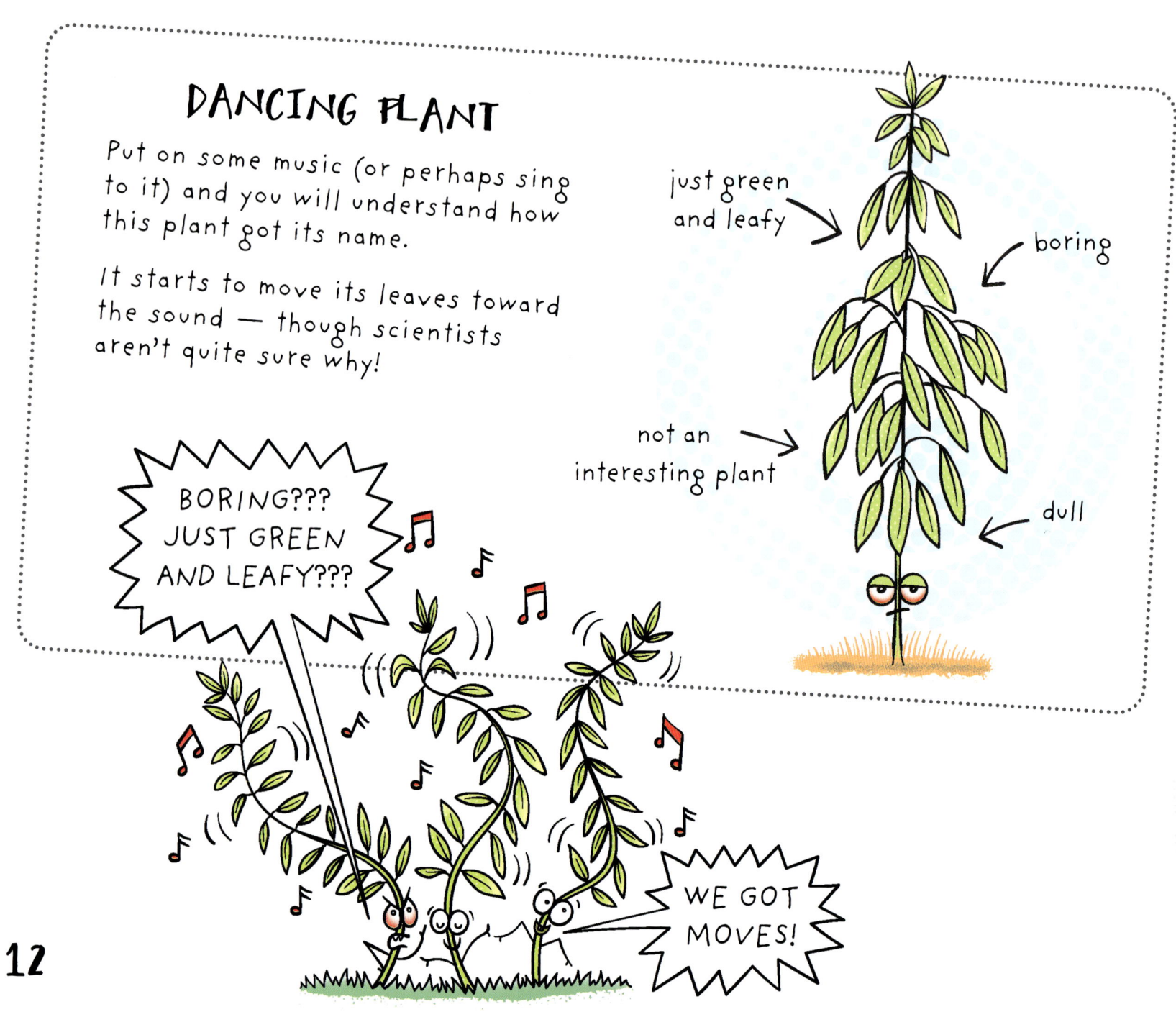

DANCING PLANT

Put on some music (or perhaps sing to it) and you will understand how this plant got its name.

It starts to move its leaves toward the sound — though scientists aren't quite sure why!

just green and leafy →

← boring

not an interesting plant →

← dull

BORING??? JUST GREEN AND LEAFY???

WE GOT MOVES!

12

SENSITIVE PLANT

This plant does NOT like being touched. Brush it, tickle it, bang into it — whatever you do, it just droops down in disappointment.

Even hungry herbivores can be put off by the suddenly saggy leaves.

WARNING! SUPER-SENSITIVE PLANT!

Should the road be here?

Here would be better.

WAHHH!

DROOP!

WAHHH!

Aw, such sensitive souls!

SLIME MOULD*

When one slime mould wants to connect to another, it grows over the whole area between them — then withdraws from everything except the most direct route.

What IS that?

*Slime moulds have their own category — not plant, not fungus, not animal. But they are too fascinating to ignore!

13

COMPLETE STINKERS

To be honest, these plants are really only funny if you're watching someone else sniff them...

TITAN ARUM

It is a good job the titan arum only flowers every few years. Its flowers absolutely stink of rotting flesh — and can be 3 metres high!

I'M BACK, BABY!

from page 4 ... and he still STINKS!

I AM hungry...

...but not THAT hungry!

If the smell of the titan arum makes you hungry, it has an edible cousin: the elephant-foot yam.

We'll have it if you don't want it!

14

CARRION (OR TOAD) PLANT

This dreadful stinker makes a smell like dead, rotting flesh. It is aiming to attract the kind of fly that enjoys that sort of smell.

SNIFF! Ahhh, delicious dead bodies!

Our favourite!

How long have you been there?

Ages! Even I'M getting sick of the smell...

Imagine being held prisoner on the stinking flower of a carrion plant.

It's the plant, honest.

I don't think it's JUST me...

DEHERAINIA SMARAGDINA

These flowers smell (REALLY smell) like cheesy feet. Or maybe whiffy blue cheese.

Mmmm — cheese!

VERY FUNNY FUNGI

Although most of us think of them as plants, fungi are actually a separate category.*

That's not what normally hatches from an egg!

OCTOPUS FUNGUS

This fungus lives mostly underground. When it wants to reproduce, though, it sends up bright-red tentacles — which stink of rotting flesh. Yeuw!

Delicious!

Disgusting!

*In fact, some experts think fungi are more closely related to animals than plants, which feels a bit creepy.

BEAR'S-HEAD TOOTH MUSHROOM

Looking more like a mop than a mushroom, this can be eaten when young. (The fungus, that is: <u>you</u> can eat it however old you are.)

Apparently they taste like lobster!

BLUE-MILK MUSHROOM

If you like colourful meals, this could be just the mushroom for you. When it is cut open, bright-blue goo leaks out.

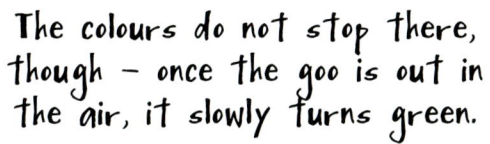

The colours do not stop there, though – once the goo is out in the air, it slowly turns green.

uncut → freshly cut → green and gooey

17

FRUIT IS FUNNY, TOO

If you're getting sick of the same two fruits on rotation in your lunch box, perhaps one of these will keep it interesting?

THE SAUSAGE TREE

You only have to see one of these to understand how it got its name*. Sausages don't grow on trees, though.

Poor thing's going to be so disappointed.

DROOL!

Light the barbeque!

*They're actually fruit, of course, and can be over a metre long!

DURIAN FRUIT

Durian is one of the most nutritious fruits in the world — it's even been dubbed the 'King of Fruits'! Its custard-like flesh is strong in vitamins — and scent.

INESCAPABLE AROMA

YOU'RE NOT FOOLING ANYONE, SIR!

But it's so tasty!

Strong-smelling durian is banned on Singapore's trains.

THE ICE-CREAM BEAN

These beans really do taste like ice cream, and they look like they are wrapped in candyfloss. All this inside a pod that can be as long as 3 metres.

I LOVE ice cream.

Imagine feeding someone beans that taste of ice cream — THAT would be funny!

TRICKSTER PLANTS

You have to feel sorry for some insects and animals — these plants give them a really hard time.

HYDNORA

This plant has no leaves, its flowers are like a gaping red mouth, and it smells rotten. Insects are drawn in by the smell — and once they're in, there's no escape!

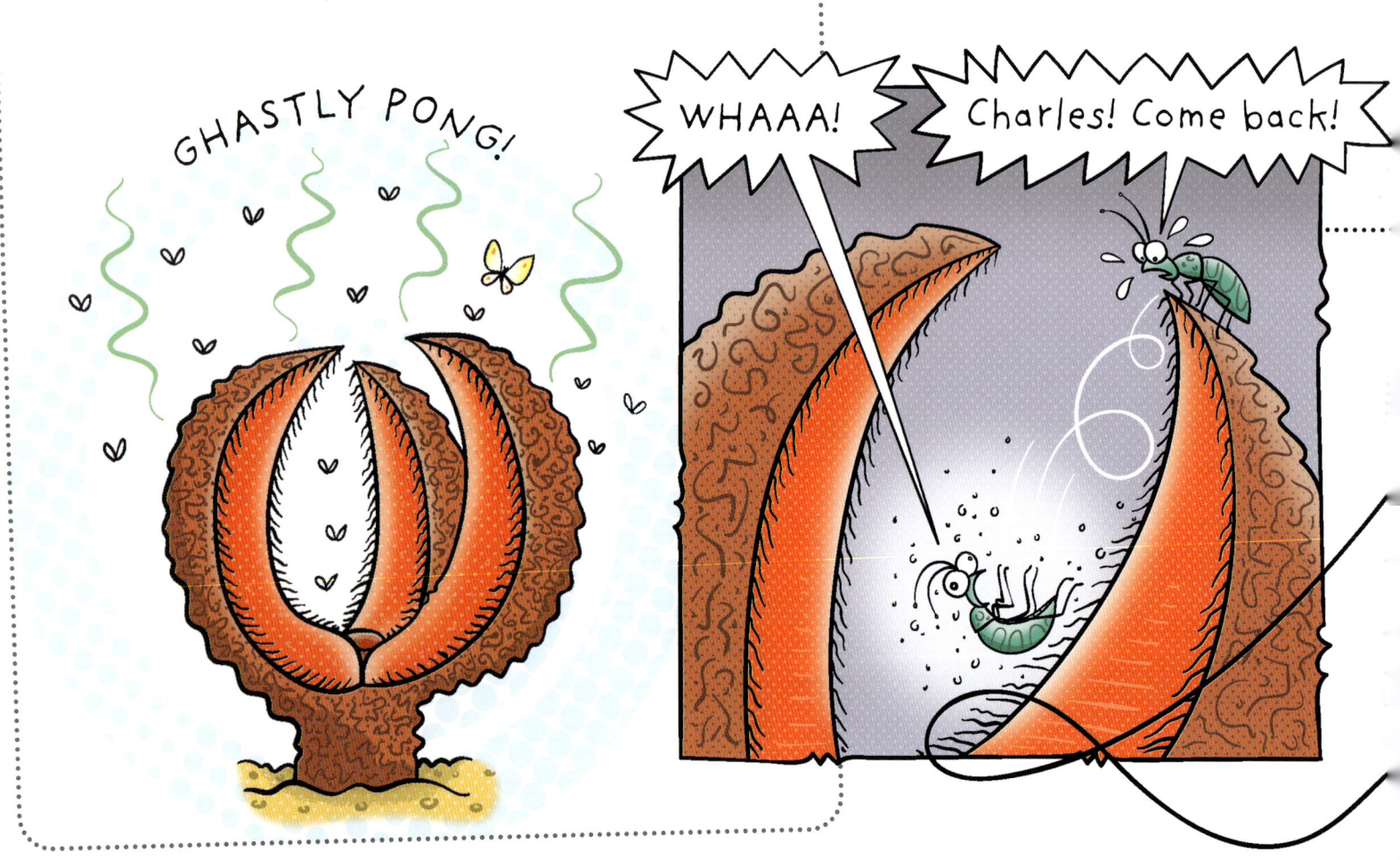

GHASTLY PONG!

WHAAA!

Charles! Come back!

20

ELEPHANT'S FOOT

This plant avoids being eaten by disguising itself as a rock.

WHOA! A LIVING ROCK!

Even when it grows flowers, they look as though they are coming from the crack between two rocks.

Hey — cool hairstyle, man!

HAMMER ORCHID

The hammer orchid grows an odd-looking appendage that looks a bit like a hammer (which is how it got its name). But this orchid wants help with pollination, not DIY.

The appendage also looks just like a (flightless) female thynnid wasp.

Ooh — hello!

I said — HELLO!

Ignore me, then!

21

SHAPELY PLANTS

Plants use the smell, shape and colour of their flowers, and sometimes fruits, to attract insects. This has led to some having very odd shapes ...

PARROT FLOWER

From the front, this just looks like a pretty flower ...

... but from the side, it suddenly looks like a parrot!

I'm NOT a parrot, though. I'm a plant.

SQUARK!

22

SNAPDRAGON

Snapdragon flowers are fun — if you squeeze them gently from the side, they open and close, a bit like a dragon's jaws.

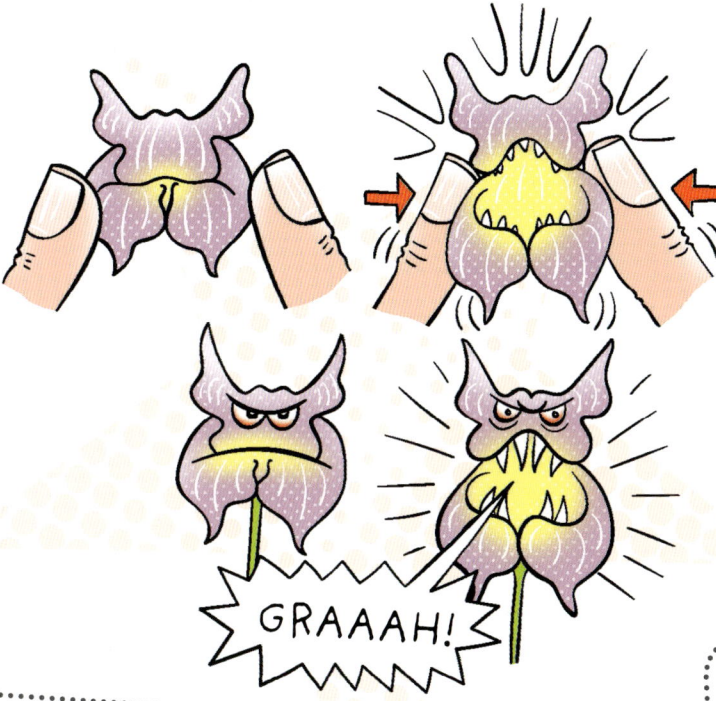

GRAAAH!

When snapdragon flowers die, the petals fall off.

WAAAH!

Left behind are seed pods that even a wasp would find worrying.

Hmm. Suddenly I want some lemon ice cream.

BUDDHA'S HAND

With its 'fingers' reaching out at you, this might just be the oddest-looking fruit on the planet. It is a citrus fruit (like lemon) and smells lovely and fresh.

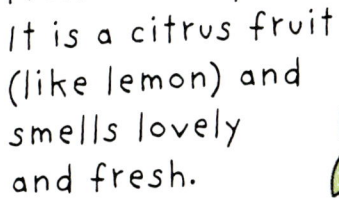

23

TERRIFIC TREES

Trees are the biggest plants on Earth. In fact, the world's tallest living thing is a coast redwood tree from California in the USA.

BAOBAB

Baobab trees grow in Africa, Madagascar and Australia. Their super-wide trunks are thought to be a way of storing water, helping the tree survive in its dry habitat.

How long did you get, mate?

Tree years.

Stories say that a baobab in Western Australia was once used as a jail.

DRAGON'S BLOOD TREE

Legend says that this tree grows where a dragon has died. This is unlikely to be true* but it does 'bleed' blood-red resin when it is cut.

Dragon's-blood resin is used in:
1) breath fresheners (which do work) and
2) love potions (which do not).

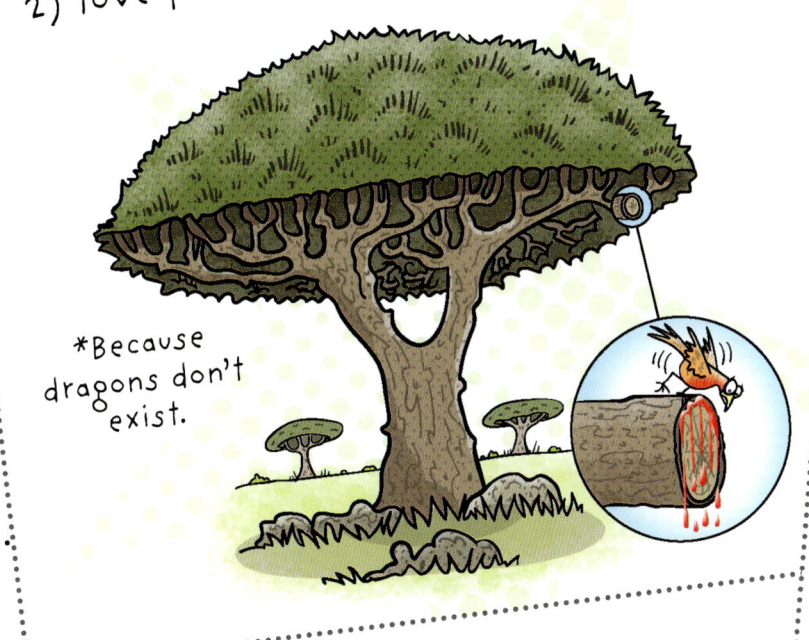

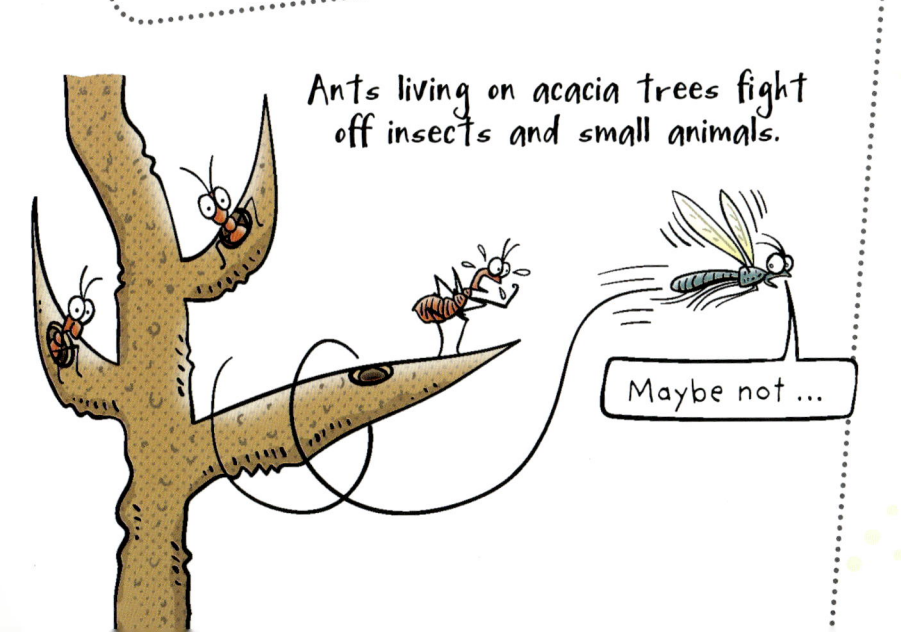

*Because dragons don't exist.

"Nice breath, but still not interested."

FRESH!

BULLHORN ACACIA

The first thing you notice about a bullhorn acacia tree is probably its thorns. These stop hungry animals from eating the leaves — and they are also home to ants.

Ants living on acacia trees fight off insects and small animals.

Maybe not...

← Spikey tree

← Spikey animal

25

PLANTS AND PEOPLE

People use plants in some funny ways — as these examples show.

CELLULOSE

Cellulose is what most plants are made of. It is also used to make something called guncotton — a very powerful explosive. This was discovered in an odd way:

In 1846 a scientist was doing an experiment in his kitchen, when he spilled some acid.

He grabbed his wife's cotton apron and mopped it up.

Disaster avoided ... until he hung the apron on the stove to dry. The cellulose in the cotton had combined with the acid to form guncotton — BOOM!

DON'T TRY THIS AT HOME.

BELLADONNA

Belladonna is deadly poisonous — but that didn't stop medieval ladies using it to dilate their pupils. They had odd ideas about beauty back then!

DON'T TRY THIS AT HOME.

"What do you think?"

"Er... lovely... you are a bella donna*!"

*'beautiful lady' in Italian.

RUBBER FIG TREE

This tree has roots that will grow through air. In northeast India, people have used the trees to make bridges. The roots are guided across a river.

"I don't like this."

"I TOLD you: we only use that when the water's too deep."

27

MORE FUNNY PLANTS

We couldn't fit all the funny plants we wanted to into the book — but here are just a few more.

DOLL'S EYES (OR WHITE BANEBERRY)

This plant has white berries with a dark spot on red stalks. It makes these plants look like a collection of plucked-out eyes looking at you.

EEK!

VEGETABLE SHEEP

This is a plant from New Zealand that looks like a sheep. From a distance.

Baaaaaack off, you!

STRANGLEWEED

This is a plant that gets its name from its thin, light-coloured strands, which hang down from tree branches.

It cannot make its own food, so it feeds off other plants.

It could be considered a vampire plant!

I want to suck your nutrients.

EEK!

SNEEZEWORT

This member of the daisy family is famous for its nicknames: stenchgrass, old man's pepper, goose tongue, nose-bleed and soldier's woundwort.

Its leaves contain a chemical that stops bleeding.

I'm multi-talented, you know.

WOLLEMI PINE

This amazing tree species most likely existed when dinosaurs walked the Earth.

I'm a survivor!

PLANTS QUIZ

1. The squirting cucumber does not like being touched. How does it let you know?

a) Shivers, shakes and generally makes a fuss.

b) Droops like a balloon with no air.

c) Explodes a sticky mess at you.

2. Which of these lights up underwater?

a) The foxfire fungus, which was used for light in early submarines.

b) Bladderwort, because it lives underwater.

c) Octopus fungus, obviously.

3. What is a ghost pipe?

a) Something used by phantom pipe smokers.

b) A plant that can grow in dark forests, without light.

c) A pipe that ghosts can travel along.

4. Which plant has been banned from Singapore's trains?

a) The snapdragon and dragonsblood tree (because no one likes to share a train with a dragon).

b) Cellulose, in case it causes a fire or explosion.

c) Durian fruit, because it smells so strong.

5. Last question: which did you think was the funniest plant in this book?

There is no right answer to this one — but all the OTHER answers are upside-down below.

Answers

1. It's c) — a) was the dancing plant and b) was the sensitive plant.

2. The answer is a) (bladderwort does live underwater, but octopus fungus just gets its name from having tentacles).

3. Ghost pipes are plants that can grow in dark forests. (The others are wrong because there's no such thing as ghosts.)

4. Durian fruit is both stinky and popular in Singapore — which is why it's banned on Singapore's trains.

30

GLOSSARY

appendage additional part that is joined to something larger

Buddha founder of the religion Buddhism

carrion rotting flesh of dead animals

chlorophyll material inside green plants that allows them to get energy from the Sun

constipation not being able to do a poo

crustacean animal with a hard, outer shell, for example a crab, shrimp or lobster

eject push out, often quickly or powerfully

fungus living thing that reproduces from spores, single cells puffed out into the air

habitat place where an animal or plant usually lives

herbivore animal that eats only plants

pollen powdery material that is released by the male parts of flowers

pollination spread of pollen to the female parts of flowers

seed produced by flowering plants, seeds are the things from which new plants grow

stalk the main stem of a plant

FURTHER READING

For more fun nature reading, why not try these other awesome books?

The **Body Bits** series, by Paul Mason and Dave Smith, Wayland 2020

- *Hair-raising Human Body Facts*
  9781526312891 Paperback
- *Astounding Animal Body Facts*
  9781526313447 Paperback
- *Eye-popping Plant Part Facts*
  9781526314659 Paperback
- *Dead-awesome Dinosaur Body Facts*
  9781526315175 Paperback

The **Animals Do** series, by Paul Mason, Tony De Saulles and Gemma Hastilow, Wayland 2018–2022

- *The Poo that Animals Do*
  9781526303950 Paperback
- *The Wee that Animals Pee*
  9781526309730 Paperback
- *The Farts that Animals Parp*
  9781526312235 Paperback
- *The Snot that Animals Have Got*
  9781526317100 Paperback

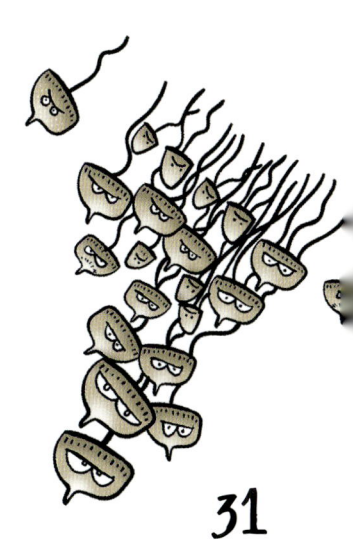

INDEX

baobab trees 24
belladonna 27
berries 28
bladderwort 11
Buddha's hand 23
bullhorn acacia 25
bunchberry dogwood 7

Cape sundew 11
carnivorous plants 10–11, 14–15, 20
carrion plant 15
cellulose 26
coast redwood 24
cucumber
    salad 5
    squirting 5, 6

dancing plant 12
Deherainia smaragdina 15
doll's eyes 28
dragon's blood tree 25

elephant's foot 21
exploding plants 6–7

fruit 18–19
    durian 19
    ice-cream bean 19

fungi 5, 8, 9, 16–17
    bear's-head tooth mushroom 17
    blue-milk mushroom 17
    foxfire 8
    mushrooms 9
    octopus 16

ghost pipe 9
guncotton 26

hydnora 4, 20

lichen 29
light 8–9

orchid, hammer 21

parrot flower 4, 22
pollen 7

roots 27
rubber fig tree 27

sausage tree 4, 18
seeds 6, 7, 23
sensitive plant 13
slime mould 13

smelly plants 5, 14–15, 16, 20
snapdragon 23
sneezewort 29
strangleweed 29

titan arum 14
touch-me-not 7
trees 24–25

vegetable sheep 28
Venus flytrap 10

white baneberry 28
wollemi pine 29

32